3
READER

Crime Scene Investigation

PIZZA

School Specialty Publishing
Columbus, Ohio

By Teresa Domnauer

Copyright © 2007 School Specialty Publishing, a member
of the School Specialty Family.

Library of Congress Cataloging-in-Publication Data is on file with the publisher.

Send all inquiries to:
School Specialty Publishing
8720 Orion Place
Columbus, OH 43240-2111

ISBN 0-7696-6381-8

1 2 3 4 5 6 7 8 9 10 PHX 11 10 09 08 07

At the scene of a crime, there are clues.
A crime scene investigator must find the clues
that will help solve the crime.
Sometimes, the clues are easy to find.
Other times, the clues are not so clear.
Many different people help
an investigator along the way.

First Responder

The first responder is the first person
to arrive at a crime scene.
A crime scene is where a crime took place.
A police officer or a firefighter
might be the first responder.
An ambulance driver or any person
who was nearby could also be
the first responder.

Weird Facts

- If someone is hurt, the first responder
  might try to help him or her.

- A crime scene can be dangerous. The
  person who committed the crime may be
  there when the first responder arrives.

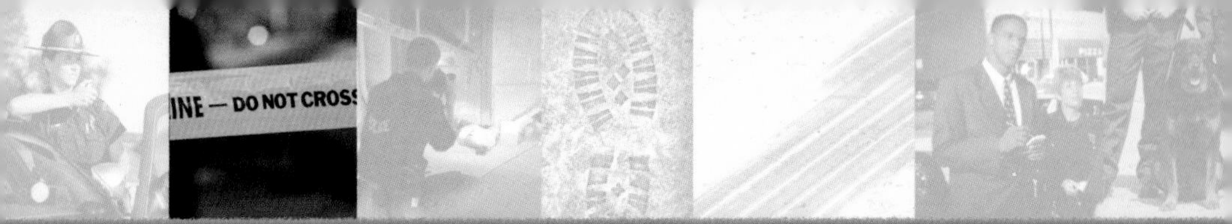

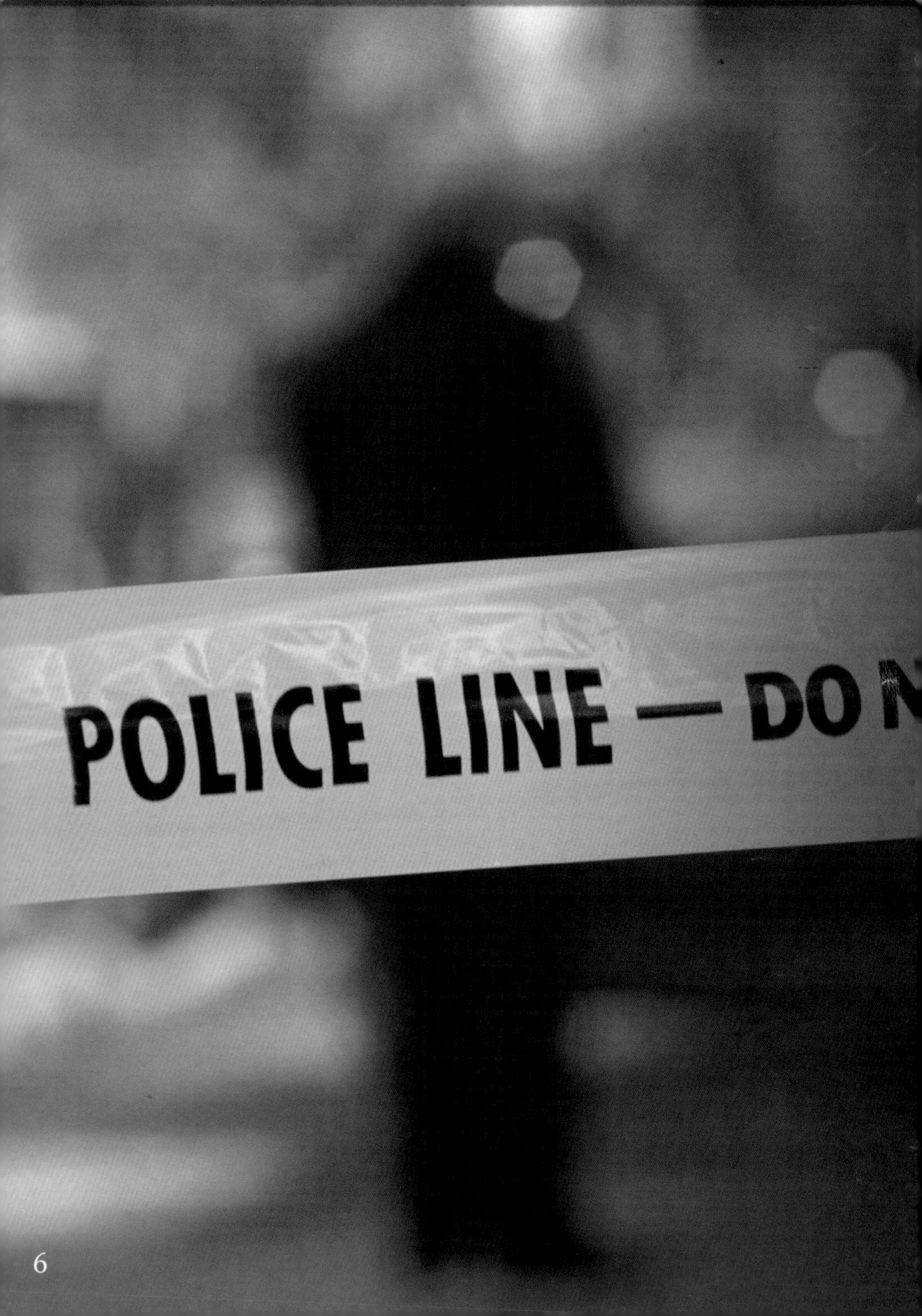
POLICE LINE — DO

Secure the Crime Scene

After a crime happens,
it is important to secure the scene.
The police hang bright yellow tape
around the area where the crime happened.
This keeps people away from the scene.
It also keeps people from moving
or damaging the evidence, or clues.

Weird Facts

- Police keep track of who enters and exits a crime scene. Then, if something happens to the scene, they know who to question about it.

- A crime scene can be as small as a closet or as large as a football field.

Photographs

It is important to have photographs of the crime scene.
Sometimes, a police officer takes the photographs.
Sometimes, a crime scene photographer takes them.
They photograph every part of the scene.
Later, they can look at the crime scene again and again in the photographs.

Weird Facts

- A crime scene is often videotaped as well as photographed.

- Crime scene investigators take written notes about the crime scene, too.

The Search for Evidence

Investigators look for evidence all around
the crime scene.
They look for anything that will tell them
who committed the crime.
Evidence can be footprints, fingerprints,
blood, or bullets.
Computers, tools, cars, and weapons
can all be evidence, too.

Weird Facts

- Before searching for evidence, investigators draw a map of the crime scene.

- If a suspect—a person who might have committed the crime—leaves a footprint, investigators can make a copy of the print.

11

Sometimes, evidence is easy to see,
such as tire tracks.
Some evidence is harder to spot.
This evidence is called *trace evidence*.
Hairs, grains of sand, and threads
from clothing are all kinds of trace evidence.
Scientists examine this evidence
under a microscope.

Weird Facts

- Investigators use a small vacuum to collect tiny pieces of glass or dirt.

- Trace evidence can also be picked up with tweezers.

Police gather other kinds of evidence, too.
They talk to people who may have seen
the crime.
These people are called *witnesses*.
Police ask the witnesses questions
about what they saw and heard.
Any kind of information can be helpful
in solving the crime.

Weird Facts

- The police find out the names and addresses of all the witnesses of the crime.

- Witnesses are not allowed to talk to each other about the crime. They might confuse one another about what they saw or heard.

Special Experts

Sometimes, dogs help investigate crimes.
Their strong sense of smell helps the police
find people.
Dogs can also sniff out drugs and explosives.
Police dogs go through special training
to do this job.

Weird Facts

- A dog has a sense of smell that is one
  million times greater than a human being's.

- Some dogs can follow trails of scent that
  are over an hour old.

Recording Evidence

Investigators collect evidence very carefully.
They wear special gloves.
They place the objects in plastic bags
and bottles.
They label each item.
They try to keep evidence clean and pure
so that it can be used in court.
Investigators want the evidence to be
exactly how it was at the crime scene.

Weird Facts

- Investigators must choose the evidence they think is the most important. They cannot pick up every single item.

- There must be a record of everything that happens to a piece of evidence.

Crime Lab

Investigators take evidence to the crime lab.
There, scientists try to find out more
about it.
They view blood or other chemicals
under a microscope.
The microscope lets scientists see
the tiniest of clues.

Weird Facts

- Scientists use special X-ray machines to look at evidence in the crime lab.

- The scientists who work in a crime lab are called *forensic scientists*.

Ballistics

Ballistics is the study of guns and bullets.
At the crime lab, experts in ballistics
look carefully at the marks on a bullet.
These marks are called *grooves*.
The grooves show an expert
which type of gun the bullet came from.

Weird Facts

- Ballistics experts can also tell the distance from which a gun was fired by looking at the bullet.

- Computers also help experts match bullets to guns.

23

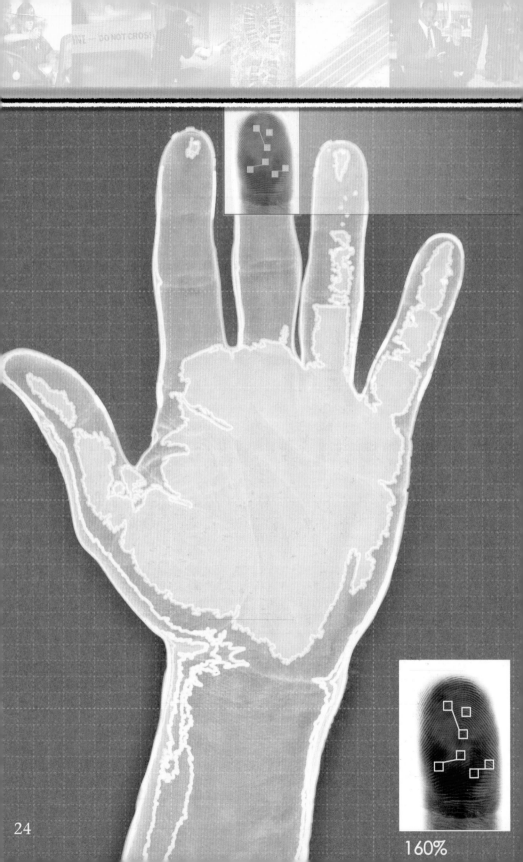

160%

Fingerprints

Sometimes, criminals leave fingerprints
at a crime scene.
It is an investigator's job to find them.
First, the investigator dusts the area
with a special powder.
Then, he or she lifts the prints with tape.
Computers search for prints that match
the ones from the crime scene.

Weird Facts

- No two people have the same fingerprints.
  Even identical twins have different
  fingerprints!

- A person's fingerprints do not change
  throughout his or her life.

Suspect

If an investigator finds enough evidence, the police can arrest a suspect.
A suspect is a person whom the police think committed the crime.
A suspect is innocent until proven guilty in a court of law.

Weird Facts

- A suspect in a serious crime may be held in jail until the trial.

- Sometimes, a suspect is placed in a police "lineup." Witnesses look at the lineup to see if they recognize anyone in it.

Detective Work

A detective is a type of investigator.
Police detectives are given
certain crimes to investigate.
They are always looking for more
information about their cases, or crimes.
They speak to many witnesses.
They ask suspects many questions.
They keep records of everything they do.

Weird Facts

- Detectives often visit places where the suspects might live or spend time.

- Crime scene investigations do not happen quickly. Some last for years and years.

Evidence in Court

Sometimes, a criminal case goes
to a court of law.
A group of people called a *jury* decides
if the suspect is innocent or guilty.
Sometimes, a judge decides.
The evidence is shown in the court.
The judge makes sure the evidence was
handled carefully.
Then, the judge makes a decision.

Weird Facts

- If evidence has not been handled carefully, the judge might not let it be used in court.

- In court, witnesses have a chance to tell what they saw happen at the crime scene.

EXTREME FACTS ABOUT CRIME SCENE INVESTIGATION!

- If the first responder at a crime scene notices any smells, he or she writes notes about them before the smells disappear.

- Sometimes, police put up tents or walls around a crime scene to secure it.

- If the crime scene is in a busy place, such as a main road, the search for evidence must take place very quickly.

- Crime scene photographers take both color and black-and-white photographs of the crime scene.

- Evidence outdoors must be collected quickly so that the weather does not destroy it.

- If a suspect has dumped evidence into a body of water, special police divers may be called in to recover it.

- Not every witness to a crime will agree to appear in court.

- Bloodhounds and German shepherds are not the only kinds of police dogs. Many other kinds of dogs can be trained for this job.

- Each piece of evidence must be placed in its own bag. Some evidence might even need to be kept in a refrigerator.

- In 1910, Frenchman Edmond Locard created the world's first crime lab.

- The serial number on a gun helps investigators find its owner, who may be a suspect.

- The FBI has several hundred million fingerprints on file.

- When police arrest a suspect, an officer must read the suspect his or her "rights." A suspect's rights include having a lawyer.

- Some police detectives wear regular clothes instead of uniforms. They are called "plainclothes" officers.

- Criminal cases are not settled in a day. Sometimes, they take weeks, months, or even years in court.